HOPE . . . *the Best of Things*

HOPE

...the Best of Things

JONI EARECKSON TADA

WHEATON, ILLINOIS

ISBN-13: 978-1-4335-0219-4
ISBN-10: 1-4335-0219-4
ePub ISBN: 978-1-4335-2233-8
PDF ISBN: 978-1-4335-0434-1
Mobipocket ISBN: 978-1-4335-0435-8

Library of Congress Cataloging-in-Publication Data

Tada, Joni Eareckson.
   Hope—the best of things / Joni Eareckson Tada.
      p. cm.
   Originally published as part of Suffering and the sovereignty of God, © 2006
   ISBN 978-1-4335-0219-4 (tpb)
   1. Tada, Joni Eareckson. 2. Hope—Religious aspects—Christianity. 3. Suffering—Religious aspects—Christianity. I. Title.
BV4638.T34   2008
241'.4—dc22   2007050383

For

Carmen Thompson

. . . WHOSE HOPE IS THE LORD

Contents

Preface

If you have picked up this booklet, it's safe to say you are interested in hope—understanding it, finding it, and resting in it. Ours is a world in terrible turmoil. People are angry; cynicism and despair are on the rise, and the nightly news reminds us we are only one terrorist plot away from another national nightmare. Oh, how we need to grasp the soul-settling hope found in the pages of God's Word—not only grasp it, but allow the hope of God to fill and overflow our hearts, transforming us into people who are confident and at peace with themselves, their God, and their circumstances.

You may not realize it, and it may seem odd, but the sufferings that are scratching at your door are the very windows through which God wants to shine his brightest rays of hope. He wants to illumine your heart with his peace, power, and perspective.

That is why I have written this special booklet, *Hope . . . the Best of Things*. For more than forty years, I have lived in a wheelchair as a spinal cord-injured quadriplegic, and believe me, I would never have made it this far were it not for the heaven-sent hope found only in Christ, the Blessed Hope. It is my prayer that the stories I share on the following pages, as well as the insights about suffering and the goodness of God, will draw you closer to him. May this little book be your guide toward a fresh, new perspective on your hardships and heartaches. I ask only that you read with prayerful expectancy as to the hope and help God desires to shine upon you this day!

Joni Eareckson Tada

1

HOPE IS HARD TO COME BY

Sometimes hope is hard to come by. Like the other week when I visited my friend Gracie Sutherlin in the hospital. Gracie has been volunteering at our Joni and Friends' Family Retreats for many years, and despite her age of sixty-one, she's always been energetic and active with the disabled children at our camps. All that changed a month ago when she broke her neck in a tragic accident. Gracie has always been happy and buoyant, but when I wheeled into the intensive care unit to visit her, I did not even recognize the woman lying in the hospital bed. With tubes running in and out of her, a ventilator shoved down her throat, and Crutchfield tongs screwed into her skull, Gracie looked completely helpless. She couldn't even breathe on her own. All she could do was open and close her eyes.

I sat there by Gracie's hospital bed. I read Scriptures to her. I sang to her: "Be still my soul, the Lord is on thy side." I leaned as far forward as I could and whispered, "Oh, Gracie, Gracie, remember. Hope is a good thing, maybe the best of things. And no good thing ever dies." She blinked at that point, and I knew she recognized the phrase. It's a line from the movie *The Shawshank Redemption*.

The Shawshank Redemption is a story about two men—Andy Dufrane, who is unjustly convicted and sentenced to life imprisonment, and his friend Red. After many hard years in prison, Andy opens up a path of promise for himself and for Red. One day in the prison yard, he instructs Red that if he is ever freed from

Shawshank, he should go to a certain town and find a certain tree in a certain cornfield, to push aside the rocks to uncover a little tin can, and to use the money in the can to make it across the border to a little Mexican fishing village. Not long after this conversation, Andy escapes from prison and Red is paroled. Red, dutiful friend that he is, finds the cornfield, the tree, the rocks, the tin can, the money—and a letter, in which Andy has written, "Red, never forget. Hope is a good thing, maybe the best of things. And no good thing ever dies." At that moment, Red realizes he has two choices: "Get busy livin' or get busy dyin'."

Sadly, right now, it appears as though my friend Gracie is busy dying. She is stuck at UCLA waiting for surgery on her neck, and an infection in her body is running rampant. The doctors are trying to get her white blood cell count down, but it doesn't look promising. Now when visitors come in to see her, she shuts her eyes against them. *Oh, Gracie, hold onto hope. It's a good thing, maybe the best of things.*

The Breaking Point

But hope is hard to come by. I should know. I remember the time when I was once busy dying. It wasn't long after I had broken my neck in a diving accident that I spent one particularly hopeless week in the hospital. I had endured long surgeries to shave down the bony prominences on my back, and it was a long recovery. I had lost a great deal of weight. And for almost three weeks I was forced to lie facedown on what's called a Stryker frame—a long, flat canvas sandwich where they put you faceup for three hours and then strap another piece of canvas on you and flip you facedown to lie there for another three hours.

Trapped facedown, staring at the floor hour after hour, my thoughts grew dark and hopeless. All I could think was, "Great, God. Way to go. I'm a brand-new Christian. This is the way you treat your new Christians? I'm young in the faith. I prayed for a closer walk with you. If this is your idea of an answer to prayer, I am never going to trust you with another prayer again. I can't believe that I have to lie facedown and do nothing but count the tiles on the floor on this stupid torture rack. I hate my existence." I asked the hospital staff to turn out the lights, close the blinds, close the door, and if anybody came in—visitor, parent, nurse—I just grunted. I justified it all. I rationalized that God shouldn't mind that I would be bitter—after all, I was paralyzed. And I didn't care how much joy was set before me. This was one cross I was not going to bear without a battle.

My thoughts got darker because no longer was my bitterness a tiny trickle. It had become a raging torrent, and in the middle of the night I would imagine God holding my sin up before my face and saying lovingly but firmly, "Joni, what are you going to do about this? What are you going to do about this attitude? It is wrong. This sin is wrong. Get rid of it." But I, hurting and stubborn, preferred my sins. I preferred my peevish, snide, small-minded, mean-spirited comments, grunting at people when they walked in or out, and letting food drool out of my mouth. Those were sins that I had made my own.

You know what it's like when you make sin your own. You housebreak it. You domesticate it. You shield it from the Spirit's scrutiny. I did not want to let go of the sick, strange comfort of my own misery.

So God gave me some help. About one week into that three-week stint of lying facedown, staring at the floor, waiting for my back to heal, I got hit with a bad case of the flu. And suddenly, not being able to move was peanuts compared to not being able to breathe. I was claustrophobic. I was suffering. I was gasping for breath. I could not move. All was hopeless. All was gone. I was falling backward, head over heels, down for the count, decimated.

And I broke. I thought, "I can't do this. I can't live this way.

I would rather die than face this." Little did I realize that I was echoing the sentiments of the apostle Paul, who in 2 Corinthians 1:8 talks of being "so utterly burdened beyond [his] strength that [he] despaired of life itself." Indeed, he even had in his heart the sentence of death. "O God, I don't have the strength to face this. I would rather die. Help me." That was my prayer. That was my anguish.

God Can Raise Us Out of Hopelessness

That week a friend came to see me in the hospital while I was still facedown counting the tiles. She put a Bible on a little stool in front of me and stuck my mouth stick in my mouth so that I could flip its pages, and my friend told me to turn to Psalm 18. There I read: "In my distress I called upon the LORD; to my God I cried for help. From his temple he heard my voice, and my cry to him reached his ears. Then the earth reeled and rocked. . . . Smoke went up from his nostrils. . . . He bowed the heavens and came down. . . . He sent from on high, he took me. . . . He rescued me"—and here's the best part—"because he delighted in me" (vv. 6–19).

I had prayed for God to help me. But little did I realize that God was parting heaven and earth, striking bolts of lightning, and thundering the foundations of the planet to reach down and rescue me because he delighted in me. He showed me in 2 Corinthians 1:9 that all this had happened so that I would "rely not on [myself] but on God who raises the dead." And that's all God was looking for. He wanted me to reckon myself dead—dead to sin—because if God can raise the dead, you'd better believe he could raise me out of my hopelessness. He would take it from there. And he has been doing the same for nearly four decades.

2

MEETING SUFFERING AND JOY ON GOD'S TERMS

*F*our decades ago, as I lay facedown and helpless, God raised me up out of hopelessness, but that was no isolated incident. I didn't just leave my desperation back there in the hospital. No, desperation is part of a quadriplegic's life each and every day. For me, suffering is still that jackhammer breaking apart my rocks of resistance every day. It's still the chisel that God is using to chip away at my self-sufficiency and my self-motivation and my self-consumption. Suffering is still that sheepdog snapping and barking at my heels, driving me down the road to Calvary where otherwise I do not want to go. My human nature, my flesh, does not want to endure hardship like a good soldier (2 Tim. 2:3) or follow Christ's example (1 Pet. 2:21) or welcome a trial as friend. No, my flesh does not want to rejoice in suffering (Rom. 5:3) or be holy as he is holy (1 Pet. 1:15). But it is at Calvary, at the cross, where I meet suffering on God's terms.

And it happens almost every morning. Please know that I am no expert at this wheelchair thing. I'm no professional at being a quadriplegic. There are so many mornings when I wake up and I can hear my girlfriend come to the front door to help me get out of bed and get ready for the day. She goes to the kitchen, turns on the water, and starts brewing coffee. I know that in a few moments she's going to come gliding into the bedroom, where she'll greet me with a happy "Good morning!" and I am lying there with my eyes closed, thinking, "Oh, God, I can't do this. I am so tired. I don't know how I'm going to make it to lunchtime. Oh, God, I'm already thinking about how good it's going to feel when I get back to bed tonight and put my head on this pillow."

I'm sure you have felt that way at some point. Maybe you feel that way every morning. But Psalm 10:17 says, "O LORD, you hear the desire of the afflicted; you will strengthen their heart; you will incline your ear." "O God," I often pray in the morning, "God, I cannot do this. I cannot do this thing called quadriplegia. I have no resources for this. I have no strength for this—but you do. You've got resources. You've got strength. I can't do quadriplegia, but I can do all things through you as you strengthen me [Phil. 4:13]. I have no smile for this woman who's going to walk into my bedroom in a moment. She could be having coffee with another friend, but she's chosen to come here to help me get up. Oh, God, please may I borrow your smile?"

And just as he promises, he hears the cry of the afflicted, and before even seven-thirty in the morning he has sent joy straight from heaven. Then, when my girlfriend comes through the door with that steaming cup of coffee, I can greet her with a happy "hello!" borrowed from God.

To This You Were Called

To this you, too, were called. To this *you* were called because Christ suffered for you, leaving *you* this kind of example that you should follow. He endured the cross for the joy that was set before him (Heb. 12:2). Should we expect to do less? So then, join me; boast in your afflictions. Delight in your infirmities. Glory in your weaknesses, for then you know that Christ's power rests in you (2 Cor. 12:9). You might be handicapped on all sides, but you're not crushed. You might be perplexed, but you're not in despair. You might be knocked down, but you're not knocked out.

Because it says in 2 Corinthians 4:7–12 that every day we experience something of the death of the Lord Jesus Christ so that, in turn, we might experience the power of the life of Jesus in these bodies of ours.

Do you know who the truly handicapped people are? They are the ones—and many of them are Christians—who hear the alarm clock go off at seven-thirty in the morning, throw back the covers, jump out of bed, take a quick shower, choke down breakfast, and zoom out the front door. They do all this on automatic pilot without stopping once to acknowledge their Creator, their great God who gives them life and strength each day. Christian, if you live that way, do you know that James 4:6 says God opposes you? "God opposes the proud, but gives grace to the humble."

And who are the humble? They are people who are humiliated by their weaknesses. Catheterized people whose leg bags spring leaks on somebody else's brand-new carpet. They are immobilized people who must be fed, cleansed, dressed, and taken care of like infants. They are once-active people crippled by chronic aches and pains. God opposes the proud but gives grace to the humble, so then submit yourselves to God. Resist the devil, who loves nothing more than to discourage you and corrode your joy. Resist him and he will flee you. Draw near to God in your affliction, and he will draw near to you (James 4:6–8). Take up your cross daily and follow the Lord Jesus (Luke 9:23).

I must qualify that last statement. Please know that when I take up my cross every day I am not talking about my wheelchair. My wheelchair is not my cross to bear. Neither is your cane or walker your cross. Neither is your dead-end job or your irksome in-laws. Your cross to bear is not your migraine headaches, not your sinus infection, not your stiff joints. That is not your cross to bear. My cross is not my wheelchair; it is my attitude. Your cross is your attitude about your dead-end job and your in-laws. It is your attitude about your aches and pains. Any complaints, any grumblings, any disputings or murmurings, any anxieties, any worries, any resentments or anything that hints of a raging torrent of bitterness—these are the things God calls me to die to daily. For when I do, I not only become like him in his death (that is, taking up my cross and dying *to* the sin that he died *for* on his cross), but the power of the resurrection puts to death any doubts, fears, grumblings, and disputings. And I get to become like him in his life. I get to experience the intimate fellowship of sharing in his sufferings, the sweetness and the preciousness of the Savior. I become holy as he is holy. O God, "you will make me full of gladness with your presence" (Acts 2:28).

And to be in God's presence is to be holy. Not to be sinless, but to *sin less*. To let suffering sandblast you to the core, revealing the stuff of which you are made. And it's never pretty, is it—the sin we housebreak and domesticate and try to make our own? No. Suffering sandblasts that stuff, leaving us bare and falling head over heels, down for the count and decimated.

Meeting Joy on God's Terms

It is when your soul has been blasted bare, when you feel raw and undone, that you can be better bonded to the Savior. And then you not only meet suffering on God's terms, but you also meet joy on God's terms. And then God—as he does every morning at seven-thirty when I cry to him out of my affliction—happily shares his gladness, his joy flooding over heaven's walls filling my heart in a waterfall of delight, which then in turn always streams out to others in a flood of encouragement, and then erupts back to God in an ecstatic fountain of praise. He gets your heart pumping for heaven. He injects his peace, power, and perspective into your spiritual being. He imparts a new way of looking at your hardships. He puts a song in your heart.

I experienced this kind of elation last year when I was in

Thailand. I am the senior disability representative with the Lausanne Committee for World Evangelization, and last year thirty-six disability ministry workers from around the world, most of them disabled themselves, gathered at the Lausanne conference in Thailand. There was a tall, beautiful African from Cameroon named Nungu Magdalene Manyi, a polio survivor who has made it her life's ambition to rescue other disabled infants who are left on riverbanks to starve to death because a disability is viewed as a curse or a bad omen by local witch doctors.

Pastor Noel Fernández, blind, using his white cane, came all the way from Cuba. Therese Swinters, another polio survivor in a wheelchair, joined us from Belgium. There was Carminha Speirs from Portugal, walking with her crutches. There we came from around the world—thirty-six of us. And we were celebrating the kinds of things I've been talking about in this chapter, how when we boast in our affliction and glory in our weaknesses, God's power is poured out upon us.

By the end of the week, we happy people, our ragtag group of disabled individuals, looked around at this conference and saw that nobody else seemed to be having fun. The conference was a bit stuffy, as conferences can be when we rehearse theology *at* one another rather than live it *with* one another. Well, our group of thirty-six was having so much fun praising the Lord that our joy just spilled out of our workshop room. It flooded down the hallway. It spilled over the hotel mezzanine level. And before we knew it, there we were in this fancy resort hotel lobby, and we were a procession of praise, singing, "We are marching in the light of God, we are marching in the light of God." I wish you could have heard me singing and seen me dancing. Our procession of praise was an audio-visual of 2 Corinthians 2:14–15: "Thanks be to God, who in Christ always leads us in triumphal procession, and through us spreads the fragrance of the knowledge of him everywhere."

You see, we are to God the fragrance of Christ. The world can't see Jesus endure suffering with grace because he's not here on earth, but you and I are. And we can fill up in our flesh what is lacking in his afflictions (Col. 1:24), and in so doing become that sweet fragrance, that perfume, that aroma of Christ to God. What a blessing, a privilege, an honor! What elation! And if I am to remind the Father of his precious Son who suffered, the apple of his eye turning brown with the rot of my sin; if I am to follow in his steps, then it is a gift to suffer alongside him, to take up my cross daily and follow him.

"Since therefore Christ suffered in the flesh, arm yourselves with the same way of thinking, for whoever has suffered in the flesh has ceased from sin" (1 Pet. 4:1). I'm so glad the apostle Peter included that, because without it we would look at suffering and think that it gives us cause for bitterness, worry, self-indulgence, or some other sin, because we have "earned it." But do not use your affliction as an excuse to sin. Rather, "whoever has suffered in the flesh has ceased from sin." So we can endure hardship like a good soldier (2 Tim. 2:3). We can welcome a trial as a friend. We can face the fiery ordeal that is about to set us ablaze (1 Pet. 4:12). We can rejoice in the hope of the glory of God (Rom. 5:2). Not only so, but we can rejoice in our sufferings because we know that suffering produces perseverance (Rom. 5:3).

3

HOPE IS CONTAGIOUS

*T*omorrow morning I will wake up, and I guarantee you I'm going to be tired, my neck is going to hurt, my back is going to ache, and I'm going to say, "O Lord God, I just cannot fly all the way across the ocean. O Lord, sixteen hours on a plane. I cannot do that. Jesus, I can't do that." But I will do it because suffering produces endurance, and endurance produces character, and character produces hope, and hope never, ever, ever disappoints us (Rom. 5:3–4). Nothing can disappoint us. Nothing can rob his joy in us, and nothing can rob our joy in him, neither height nor depth nor things to come nor things past nor muscular dystrophy nor osteogenesis imperfecta, not spinal cord injury, or multiple sclerosis (Rom. 8:39), for all things are yours (1 Cor. 3:21). For you are of Christ, and Christ is of God (1 Cor. 3:23). Therefore, you can be sorrowful yet always rejoicing; you can have nothing and yet possess everything (2 Cor. 6:10).

Passing on the Hope to Others

We are so rich. We've been given so much insight, so much knowl-edge. And to whom much is given, much shall be required; to whom much is entrusted, much shall be demanded (Luke 12:48). I may have a wheelchair, but there is a need for eighteen million wheelchairs around the world. So I cannot sit here in America on my backside and be content. No. Ken and I will head to Africa with our *Wheels for the World* team to deliver not only terrain-appropriate wheelchairs, but also Bibles, and to give the good news and to teach disability ministry training in churches and to let people there know that cerebral palsy is not a curse from a local witch doctor. We will shed the light of Jesus who always tells the truth—not only about redemption but about rickets, not only about the atonement but about autism. We will shine his light. The way I see it, I've been given so much, I must pass on the blessing. We simply must, must pass on the hope to others.

We must pass on the hope to people like Gracie, with her eyes shut in UCLA, at this point perhaps hoping that God will take her home before that operation. To people like her and to people like Beverly and Ron. Beverly is a woman who wrote me the following e-mail a while back:

Dear Joni,

I'm out of hope. And I am hoping you might be able to help my husband, Ron, who was in an accident last year.

My husband is a pastor. The accident left him a quadriplegic. When he came home from the hospital he continued to pastor from his wheelchair, but then two months later he was back in the hospital with an infection. And there have been many infections since then and many visits to the hospital. My husband, Ron, began to become depressed. He has now resigned from his church, and he does not get out of bed. He does not talk. And if he answers a question, he only says, "I don't know."

I am at a loss. He does not want the lights on in his room and no TV. He does not want to live, and he does not care about our family. We have no medical insurance. We all seem to be falling through the cracks. My husband feels useless and hopeless. We need help.

How do you respond to something like that? Well, I responded by dialing 411 and tracking down Ron and Beverly's phone num-

ber. I gave them a call, Beverly answered, and I shared with her
that I had received her e-mail. I talked and prayed with her over
the phone. Finally I asked, "Any chance your husband, Ron, might
want to talk to a fellow quadriplegic?" She was delighted that I
was even interested. She knocked on his door, and he allowed her
to tuck the phone receiver under his ear. And although he would
not respond, I talked a little bit of shop about quadriplegia. I
talked about urinary infections and bowel problems and difficul-
ties breathing, and I thought I detected a grunt on the other end.

Count It All Joy . . .

I wanted to move beyond those topics, however, and bridge the
conversation to spiritual things. I thought, "This man's a pastor.
Surely he knows the Word of God." So I started to share with
him several favorite Scriptures that have sustained me through
the toughest of times:

> Count it all joy, my brothers, when you meet trials of various
> kinds, for you know that the testing of your faith produces stead-
> fastness. And let steadfastness have its full effect, that you may be
> perfect and complete, lacking in nothing. (James 1:2–4)
>   For I consider that the sufferings of this present time are
> not worth comparing with the glory that is to be revealed to us.
> (Rom. 8:18)

Still silence on the other end. I even sang to him. Nothing. Finally
I did the only thing I could think of that I hadn't already tried.
I asked Ron if he had ever seen a movie called *The Shawshank
Redemption*.

"Why, yes, I have," he said.

I couldn't believe it. He had responded. So I went on, "Well,
Ron, do you remember when Red found Andy Dufrane's letter?
Do you remember what it said?"

"I . . . I think so. 'Hope is a good thing, maybe the best of things. And no good thing ever dies.'"

"Ron, there are ten thousand other quadriplegics like you and me across America, not to mention who knows how many beyond the borders of this country. And all of them were lying in bed this morning wondering whether or not they should get busy living or get busy dying. Ron, I'm going to make a choice to get busy living. Do you want to join me today?"

"Yes, ma'am. Yes, I do."

"Good for you, Ron, because now you're in the fellowship of sharing not only my suffering but Christ's sufferings. And he'll give you the grace one day at a time. Sufficient unto this day are the evil and the trials and the troubles that you're going to face."

He put his wife back on the phone, and I proceeded to tell her about our Family Retreats. I asked, "Beverly, do you think you could get your husband Ron to one of our Family Retreats?" I promised her that our office would provide scholarship money, which we always do to families who are struggling with medical expenses. And sure enough, that summer, Ron and Beverly went to a Joni and Friends Family Retreat in Texas. Shortly after they returned home, I received another e-mail from Beverly:

Dear Joni,

Ron asked me to be sure and write you because this past month has been wonderful. Camp was a huge blessing, and I don't think we realized how much of a blessing it was until we got home. We have made new friends for a lifetime. Ron wants to find things that he can do which will get him out of the house more. I told him that whenever he's ready we can hook up our camper to our truck and go minister so he can share his testimony all over the United States. For the first time in a year he did not say no. He grinned. Thank you. We have hope.

"Hope is a good thing, maybe the best of things. And no good thing ever dies." But we live in a dark, diseased world under the curse of sin. Hell is real. And God owes this utterly rebellious planet absolutely nothing. But aren't you glad that he is a God of love, not wanting anyone to perish? And he is out to convince this unbelieving, sarcastic, skeptical world of his power to save, his abilities to sustain, and his desire to share his hope.

4

MISERY MAY LOVE COMPANY BUT JOY CRAVES A CROWD

*W*e have been given so much. Jesus said, "To you it has been given to know the secrets of the kingdom of heaven" (Matt. 13:11). And "everyone to whom much was given, of him much will be required, and from him to whom they entrusted much, they will demand the more" (Luke 12:48). God mandates that we go out into the streets and the alleys and the highways and the byways. He mandates that we find the poor, the blind, the disabled, and the lame, and help them get busy living, because misery might love company, but joy craves a crowd. And the Father and the Son and the Holy Spirit crave a crowd of joy, joy spilling over and splashing and filling the hearts of thirsty people in this world who are absolutely dehydrated from a lack of hope. They need help from God on high.

The Father and the Son and the Holy Spirit's plan is to rescue humans. The Father is gathering a crowd, an inheritance that is pure and perfect and blameless, to join him in the river of joy and the whirlwind of pleasure. And he is heaven-bent on gathering glad and happy souls who will make it their eternal ambition to worship his Son in the joy of the Holy Spirit. God is love. And the wish of love is to drench with delight those who have stepped into the fellowship of sharing in his Son's suffering.

And soon, perhaps sooner than we think, the Father, the Son, and the Holy Spirit are going to get their wish. Perhaps sooner than we think, God will close the curtain on sin and suffering and disease and death, and we are going to step into the Niagara Falls of joy that will be.

And one day I'm going to leave this wheelchair behind. I cannot wait. I may have suffered with Christ on earth, but one day in heaven I'm going to reign with him. I may have tasted the pains of living on this planet, but one day I'm going to eat from the tree of life in the pleasure of heaven, and it's all going to happen in the twinkling of an eye. Like C. S. Lewis once hinted, the Lord's overcoming of this world will be the lifting of the curtain on our five senses, and we shall see him and we shall be like him, and we shall see the whole universe in plain sight.

The Joy Set before Us

The joy-filled shock of being glorified may seem odd at first, but after we rub our arms and face, after we jump up and down a few times and kick up our heels, we'll feel right at home in our new bodies. We'll spread our arms wide and feel utterly drenched with delight. Then we'll stand amazed, looking around and laughing and feeling as though we were born for such a place—because we were!

I will look up. And walking toward me will be my husband, Ken. I know he loves me on earth, but I am just a hint, an omen, a foreshadowing of the Joni that I'll be in heaven. And when he sees me he'll say, "So this is what I loved about you all those years on earth." And I will see Ron and Beverly striding toward me, their souls' capacities stretched because of suffering, stretched for joy and pleasure and worship and service in heaven. Their souls will be large and spacious because they chose to boast in their affliction rather than wallow in sadness and self-pity.

It is my prayer that Jesus will look at Gracie and he will say to her, "I know you. You came to me hemorrhaging human strength, and I felt power go out of me, and I touched you and gave you grace upon grace upon grace."

Beyond Compare

Romans 8:18 says that we can consider our present sufferings not worth comparing with the glory that will be revealed in us. I have shared this before, but I must say it again. For I sure hope I can bring this wheelchair to heaven. Now, I know that's not theologically correct. But I hope to bring it and put it in a little corner of heaven, and then in my new, perfect, glorified body, standing on grateful glorified legs, I'll stand next to my Savior, holding his nail-pierced hands. I'll say, "Thank you, Jesus," and he will know that I mean it, because he knows me. He'll recognize me from the fellowship we're now sharing in his sufferings. And I will say, "Jesus, do you see that wheelchair? You were right when you said that in this world we would have trouble, because that thing was a *lot* of trouble. But the weaker I was in that thing, the harder I leaned on you. And the harder I leaned on you, the stronger I discovered you to be. It never would have happened had you not given me the bruising of the blessing of that wheelchair."

Then the real ticker-tape parade of praise will begin. And all of earth will join in the party.

And at that point Christ will open up our eyes to the great fountain of joy in his heart for us beyond all that we ever experienced on earth. And when we're able to stop laughing and crying, the Lord Jesus really will wipe away our tears. I find it so poignant that finally at the point when I do have the use of my arms to wipe away my own tears, I won't have to, because God will.

Hope may well be the greatest of things, because Romans 5:2 says, "We rejoice in the hope of the glory of God." I get so excited thinking about how Jesus and the Father and the Holy Spirit are anticipating on tiptoe that wonderful day when we the bride of Christ, spotless and pure and blameless, will join them and swim with them in their river of pleasure. I rejoice in that hope—the hope of God's being glorified in himself and our getting a chance to join him. The hope we wait for is our only hope, the blessed hope, the glorious appearing of our great God and Savior, Jesus Christ (Titus 2:13). It is Jesus for whom we have prevailed through all of this suffering, and, oh, for the sweetness of melding one heart into his in that intimacy that is so precious.

Is hope *really* all that hard to come by? I don't think so. Our hope is for the Desire of the nations. Our hope is the Healer of broken hearts, the Friend of sinners, the God of all encouragement, the Father of all comfort, the Lord of all hope. And it is my prayer that the eyes of your heart might be enlightened so that you might know this hope to which he has called you.

Epilogue

Thank you for taking time to read the insights on Christian hope in this special booklet. Yet there's so much more to say. And so many more people I would love for you to meet—people who are suffering many challenges yet learn to persevere in the hope of Christ.

This is why I encourage you to visit us at the Joni and Friends International Disability Center. Our staff and volunteers provide exceptional programs and services for families affected by disability, not to mention disability ministry training in churches across the country. If you or a family member is struggling to come to grips with a disabling injury or illness, I invite you to contact us and learn more about the practical and spiritual help which can be yours today.

Because no one—absolutely no one—should suffer alone. It's why God created spiritual community. And it's why our goal at the Joni and Friends International Disability Center is to help people like *you*.

For more information on other resources
related to disability issues, please contact:
Joni and Friends International Disability Center
P.O. Box 3333
Agoura Hills, CA 91376
818/707-5664
www.joniandfriends.org

Joni Eareckson Tada is Founder and CEO of the Joni and Friends International Disability Center. Through programs of practical encouragement and spiritual help, Joni and her team minister to thousands of disabled people and their families across the United States and around the world.

For more details, visit Joni's website at joniandfriends.org, or you can write to her at Joni and Friends, Post Office Box 3333, Agoura Hills, California 91376.